Great Reviews from Readers

I think the series is wonderful and beneficial for tourists to get information before visiting the city.

-Seckin Zumbul, Izmir Turkey

I am a world traveler who has read many trip guides but this one really made a difference for me. I would call it a heartfelt creation of a local guide expert instead of just a guide.

-Susy, Isla Holbox, Mexico

New to the area like me, this is a must have!

-Joe, Bloomington, USA

This is a good series that gets down to it when looking for things to do at your destination without having to read a novel for just a few ideas.

-Rachel, Monterey, USA

Good information to have to plan my trip to this destination.

-Pennie Farrell, Mexico

Great ideas for a port day.

-Mary Martin USA

Aptly titled, you won't just be a tourist after reading this book. You'll be greater than a tourist!

-Alan Warner, Grand Rapids, USA

Thank you for a fantastic book.

-Don, Philadelphia, USA

Even though I only have three days to spend in San Miguel in an upcoming visit, I will use the author's suggestions to guide some of my time there. An easy read - with chapters named to guide me in directions I want to go.

-Robert Catapano, USA

Great insights from a local perspective! Useful information and a very good value!

-Sarah, USA

This series provides an in-depth experience through the eyes of a local. Reading these series will help you to travel the city in with confidence and it'll make your journey a unique one.

-Andrew Teoh, Ipoh, Malaysia

GREATER THAN A TOURIST –

SPLIT CROATIA

50 Travel Tips from a Local

Elizabeth Pozar

Greater Than a Tourist- Split Croatia Copyright © 2018 by CZYK Publishing LLC. All Rights Reserved.

All rights reserved. No part of this book may be reproduced in any form or by any electronic or mechanical means including information storage and retrieval systems, without permission in writing from the author. The only exception is by a reviewer, who may quote short excerpts in a review.

Cover designed by: Lisa Rusczyk Ed. D.
Image: https://pixabay.com/en/croatia-split-mountains-coast-1611128/

Greater Than a Tourist
Visit our website at www.GreaterThanaTourist.com

Lock Haven, PA
All rights reserved.
ISBN: 9781982959548

>TOURIST
50 TRAVEL TIPS FROM A LOCAL

BOOK DESCRIPTION

Are you excited about planning your next trip?

Do you want to try something new?

Would you like some guidance from a local?

If you answered yes to any of these questions, then this Greater Than a Tourist book is for you.

Greater Than a Tourist – Split, Croatia by Elizabeth Pozar offers the inside scoop on Split. Most travel books tell you how to travel like a tourist. Although there is nothing wrong with that, as part of the Greater Than a Tourist series, this book will give you travel tips from someone who has lived at your next travel destination.

In these pages, you will discover advice that will help you throughout your stay. This book will not tell you exact addresses or store hours but instead will give you excitement and knowledge from a local that you may not find in other smaller print travel books.

Travel like a local. Slow down, stay in one place, and get to know the people and the culture. By the time you finish this book, you will be eager and prepared to travel to your next destination.

TABLE OF CONTENTS

BOOK DESCRIPTION
TABLE OF CONTENTS
DEDICATION
ABOUT THE AUTHOR
HOW TO USE THIS BOOK
FROM THE PUBLISHER
OUR STORY
WELCOME TO
> TOURIST
INTRODUCTION
1. Croatian Language
2. Diocletian's City
3. Same Location, Different Countries
4. Diocletian's Palace
5. View From Riva
6. Grgur Ninski Statue
7. Local Cuisine
8. Learn To Cook Like A Local
9. Hidden Restaurants
10. Eating Healthy
11. Fritule, Uštipci & Pancakes
12. Nutella
13. Ice Cream

14. Big on Wine
15. Brands Of Beer
16. Try Local Alcohol
17. World Food Brands
18. We Love Coffee
19. Are You a Smoker?
20. Coast Line Beaches
21. Bačvice
22. Bus, Taxi, Uber
23. Rent transportation
24. Where To Sleep?
25. Camping
26. Theatres
27. Enjoy Our History
28. Are You an Art Lover?
29. Our Music
30. Singers And Bands
31. Live Music And DJs
32. Ultra Music Festival
33. "The Sportiest City In The World"
34. How Should You See The City?
35. Buy At "Pazar"
36. Shopping
37. Life in the Center
38. Take A Stroll Through Our Parks
39. We Have a Volcano

40. City of Dog Lovers
41. Parking Problems
42. Game Of Thrones
43. Outside the City
44. Local Islands
45. Excursions
46. Olive Picking
47. Some Local Phrases
48. Important to Remember
49. Last Minute Advice
50. Information Online

TOP REASONS TO BOOK THIS TRIP

50 THINGS TO KNOW ABOUT PACKING LIGHT FOR TRAVEL

Packing and Planning Tips

Travel Questions

NOTES

DEDICATION

This book is dedicated to my Dad whose creative nature lives through me and hopefully brings him pride from where he is; and to my Mom for always having patience with who I am and finally to Split, which despite some of our differences always welcomes me back when I need it to.

ABOUT THE AUTHOR

Elizabeth Pozar is a Split native where she lives even today, with carefully planned on journey she has yet to take. She's a writer with a bachelor degree in journalism and a passion for writing stories. Proud puppy mom with a love for travels she has yet to immerse herself in and cooking.

She's lived in Zagreb and Mostar throughout her young adulthood due to schooling, providing her with a personal understanding of what makes Split unique in regards to cities in the region. She prefers cities but will gladly relax away from the city hype in more rural areas. Her next plan includes exploring the emerald island of Ireland.

Born and raised in Split not quite on purpose but due to circumstances of the time in which she was born, she loves meeting new people and chatting with visitors of the city to get their perspective on it, allowing her also to clue them into its secrets because she's simply never been a fan of the tourist travel and organized sightseeing. To her, cities have souls and those souls have to be explored differently.

HOW TO USE THIS BOOK

The Greater Than a Tourist book series was written by someone who has lived in an area for over three months. The goal of this book is to help travelers either dream or experience different locations by providing opinions from a local. The author has made suggestions based on their own experiences. Please do your own research before traveling to the area in case the suggested places are unavailable.

FROM THE PUBLISHER

Traveling can be one of the most important parts of a person's life. The anticipation and memories that you have are some of the best. As a publisher of the Greater Than a Tourist book series, as well as the popular 50 Things to Know book series, we strive to help you learn about new places, spark your imagination, and inspire you. Wherever you are and whatever you do I wish you safe, fun, and inspiring travel.

Lisa Rusczyk Ed. D.
CZYK Publishing

OUR STORY

Traveling is a passion of the "Greater than a Tourist" series creator. Lisa studied abroad in college, and for their honeymoon Lisa and her husband toured Europe. During her travels to Malta, an older man tried to give her some advice based on his own experience living on the island since he was a young boy. She was not sure if she should talk to the stranger but was interested in his advice. When traveling to some places she was wary to talk to locals because she was afraid that they weren't being genuine. Through her travels, Lisa learned how much locals had to share with tourists. Lisa created the "Greater Than a Tourist" book series to help connect people with locals. A topic that locals are very passionate about sharing.

WELCOME TO
> TOURIST

INTRODUCTION

*Life begins at the end of your
comfort zone.
– Neale Donald Walsch*

All journeys require the first step to be made so any travel therefore requires preparation. Split is a city full of wonders, history, people and discovery but before you get on your plane or boat, be sure to read up on it. Read online about what you will find in the city and out of it, read about our history, explore online maps and get yourself familiar with some important locations, not just the ones you want to see but also that you don't (like hospitals and police). Music is also a great place to start because we're very proud of our musicians and the music they create which will either tell you a lot about us or yourself.

Whether you prefer to stay in hotels or private accommodation, we got you covered. "Booking" website is big here so check it out; the reviews from previous guests are absolutely the best help you can get when choosing. If you're looking to be in the hype of everything, the city center (can be referred to as Old Town) or within short distance of it for slightly cheaper but still close renting.

Eat where you want to eat but don't leave without trying our local foods or checking out the vendors inside the center because you haven't really tasted Split unless you've tried our fish, meat delicacies or even tasted our wine and fruit brandies.

Dare yourself to try new things and explore, trust your maps to never stray you from where you want to go but don't limit yourself to just tourist points because then you might miss out on really seeing Split or even getting to know us.

This book will guide you through a lot of things, teach you basics and clue you in on some of the things we're really proud about but it's only the beginning of your adventure in Split. Not even all locals know everything and not all locals have seen every part of the city (some might have). We have stories and we have a lot to say, you'll like our stories. We've been in one place for centuries but we've been through plenty of rulers and countries, of which older people will have lots to say about that. It's why we have so much to offer to you.

So, whether you're looking for a new place to explore or making Split a stop on a longer journey, take it from a local that it's completely worth seeing and even coming back to.

1. CROATIAN LANGUAGE

Before we can dive into any sort of discussion about Split, we should probably sort through some details that may be confusing upon your arrival. Primary language in Croatia is the Croatian language, which is part of the Slavic group of languages (Serbian, Bosnian, Slovenian and even Russian are some examples of this). We're adapting to be easily accessible to our tourists but we still have a long way to go.

Don't be discouraged if you see any of the following letters: ć, č, dž, đ, š, ž. these are a little more unique letters, which with some thought can easily interpreted. Ć and Č for example you can find when you say English words such as **change** or **chalk**. Dž and Đ can be easily pounced when thinking of names like **Jack** or **George**. To us, these changes mean plenty but to a foreigner, it may be more confusing than anything else. Š is like the beginning of **short** and Ž you can hear in the French name **Jacques**.

Now that we've gotten that out of the way, here are some words and phrases that may come up. Some of those words aren't that far from their Croatian counterparts even: **Policija** (police), **Bolnica** (hospital), **Vatrogasci** (firefighters), **Ulica** (street), **Muzej** (museum), **Trajekt** (ferry), **Promet** (traffic and part of the name of our bus company "Promet Split"), **Kafić** (coffee shop), **Soba** (room), **Otok** (island), **Trajektna luka** (Ferry harbor), **Željeznički kolodvor** (train station), **Autobusni kolodvor** (bus station).

Within the center, a lot of the signs have already been converted to include or exclusively use English translation while some have the appropriate symbol to relate the location. Croatian words which are the same or very similar as that in English are as one would expect (hotel, hostel, **restoran** / restaurant). Outside of the center, the signs tend to be in Croatian still but they will point in the right direction.

2. DIOCLETIAN'S CITY

We should first talk about what is considered to be the birth of Split. **Roman Emperor Diocletian** ruled from his city Salona (today Solin), which isn't far from here. What is now regarded as the second largest city of Croatia was actually built as the retirement residence which is often forgotten if the massiveness of the palace is considered. Salona was the capital of the province, Split was meant to be a palace to be used in the Emperor's old age but instead, Split became a booming, ever-growing center whereas Salona is a smaller city located close by.

Today, the space which was Spalato is only a very small portion of the city but often the most interesting. Tourists often flock right here, guided by expert talkers who lead them through streets and describe our rich history which is great and certainly worth the listen but as someone who grew up in this very city and learned much of this in school rather than from a tour guide, I can tell you that the Palace is not just official stories and relevant areas. There is a beauty which the Romans bestowed upon it, depth and even wonder.

Earlier history of the city is often discarded in favor of the more famous one so if you have interest in the earlier eras, you should look into the Greek colony of **Spálathos** or even our **Illyrian tribes**.

3. SAME LOCATION, DIFFERENT COUNTRIES

If you spend a little more time in Split, you will undoubtedly realize that while the Romans build the

Palace, they were not the only influence the city faced throughout the centuries. The City had been under different rules. Some of those include Byzantians, Kingdom of Hungary, Venetian influence (particularly important as a time when our renowned **Marko Marulić** lived and created his famous work Judita), Habsburg Monarchy, Napoleon's Kingdom of Italy, and all this before the Yugoslavian eras in the previous century.

Whether history interests you or not to explore all this out, you should know that the World War II time and everything after is still a very active topic all around Croatia, including Split. During the war, we were formally under what is known as the Independent State of Croatia while its claim to victory comes from the partisan party which gave way to the creation of Yugoslavia. The always activate debate is really just about which of these was worse, who were the real villains and such. We won't be getting into this now so more take it as a warning that if it comes up, it could get interesting.

4. DIOCLETIAN'S PALACE

Peristyle is regarded as probably the most beautiful area and you should certainly go there. It's large, will lead you to the **Cathedral of Saint Duje** (and its magnificent tower) but challenge yourself not to stay there but instead follow the small streets because therein lie the many hidden gems of the palace. For example, if you take either side of the massive stairs from the Peristyle, you arrive into a beautiful circular chamber without a roof, the **Vestibul**, with flooring often showing you traces of rainbow when the sun is high enough.

If you instead choose to go to the small passage opposite of the street, you will enter a short corridor; find the small Church of St. John with beautifully crafted animals guarding it. Keep going though. Just below the sculpture, a small passage leads you on. We, locals, refer to this small space as **pusti me da prođem** (Croatian for *let me pass*). The space itself isn't so small, quite comfortable actually, but it's certainly a fun little tidbit.

The Peristyle will also lead you into the Diocletian's basements. The setting is vast and filled with many souvenirs, including jewelry. Tourists tend to spend time there quite a bit and you can always find things to take home but while you're there, you can keep exploring the Palace as well because the way it was built; there are always interesting places to discover.

The possibilities of what you can see in the Palace though are endless. The best tip to be given about the Palace is: *go* and *walk*. Explore and find those gems because whether you've seen the pictures or you've read about it, there is always so much that can be seen with your own eyes.

5. VIEW FROM RIVA

Diocletian's basements lead you to discover our Riva, a large stretch of space with views to the Adriatic Sea, filled with coffee shops and restaurants. It's only in the recent years that the area has been completely redone, but what you have here is a pleasant walk where in the sunny days there is a special sparkle to the white tiles.

Almost the whole stretch closer to the wall is covered with outside seating while on the outside; the main flooring of the area is a wide walking area. Locals consider the pricing there a little too much and tend to sit in other areas but it's really about the view. Beyond the wide path, there are a lot of benches for the viewing pleasures, with the harbor to the left and **West Coast** to the right. The latter has recently been redone as well, which would allow for a delightful stroll and if you're into photography, the West Coast offers a good view of the Palace.

6. GRGUR NINSKI STATUE

Each side of the Palace had gates, each of them named. Golden Gate was one of these gates, exiting the Palace towards to the statue of **Grgur Ninski** (Gregory of Nin), a bishop during the Middle Ages, important to Croats because of his opposition to the Church and introduction of Croatian language into religious services.

The tall statue stands at the top of the stairs. There is a local tradition where one of the statue's toes is large and it is believed that if you hold it and make a wish, it will come true.

7. LOCAL CUISINE

Arguing who has the best food is possibly one that would never end because when it comes to Split, we have a lot of great restaurants. To be perfectly honest, our Moms probably cook the best but that's beside the point.

Primary diet among the locals is fish and seafood (shrimps, crabs, different clamps etc.) so you will often be able to find that type of food where you eat, even if the menu includes pizza. We also have a fish market located in the Marmont's walk, not too far from Riva. The smell of the fish is often a good guide to its location.

You should definitely try our **Dalmatinska paštica** which in its original recipe should be prepared from either veal or beef though it's important that a rougher part of the animal's leg is used and that the side dish is gnocchi. Nothing beats homemade gnocchi but the overall meal is quite delicious.

There are plenty more delicacies that are traditional in Split, also pastries that are quite common. For example, try the **burkifla** which is a puff pastry with a walnut taste to it. In restaurants, try the **rožata** which the French call Crème Caramel.

8. LEARN TO COOK LIKE A LOCAL

Dalmatians are big on cooking. They cook, bake, grill... mothers pass down recipes to their children and the cycle always continues. It's however been shown that foreigners like our cooking too so local chefs are offering cooking classes for tourists.

With a quick search online, you could find cooking classes and take home some great recipes. Speaking of recipes though, it's become quite popular to share your knowledge online so you can find *a lot* of recipes for the same dish online if you want to try it out for yourself.

9. HIDDEN RESTAURANTS

Big, small, hidden or out in the open completely, Split has no shortage of neither fine dining nor fast food these days. Inside the Palace, you will find restaurants on any corner and these days, the only competition they have is in private accommodation. The food is great and mixed; you will find pizza, pasta, meat and fish. Our restaurants don't like to limit themselves.

Try to remember that while you can easily find restaurants in the city center, you should also consider looking online for other places to eat because in Split, there's food in a lot of the areas so it really depends on what kind of view you'd like. You can eat within the palace walls, further away but still have a good view of the sea or you can go into more hidden gems and eat in older, established restaurants that may be a little off the path.

We're getting a lot better at reviewing our restaurants and tourists are certainly teaching us that so feel free to browse the web for websites like Foursquare or Tripadvisor.

10. EATING HEALTHY

Split is following the world trends when it comes to food (even if we love our meat) so the healthy food industry is slowly growing. You can find Vegan and Vegetarian restaurants here if that's your flavor or places that simply refer to themselves as health food restaurants.

In addition, the industry of health stores is booming. Bio & Bio stores are growing in numbers (one is in the city center but others are in the shopping centers) and you can also find more locally owned stores such as Makrovega, Zdravi Đir (best translated as "healthy style") and many others. This is also another thing that can be easily found on online maps.

11. FRITULE, UŠTIPCI & PANCAKES

While fast food is everywhere nowadays, more and more local pastry experts are opening food stands throughout the center where you can taste food like **fritule** or **uštipci**, flour-based pastries cooked in oil, the first are small and round, served in a tall plastic cup while the second are very long.

With **fritule** you can experiment with what you add like sugar, chocolate or even some other liquid additions but with **uštipci**, it's best if you either try it without anything or with a bit of sugar on top. It's best to eat both when they're freshly done and still warm.

Pancakes (thin variety) are big in Croatia and recently, they've become a popular food choice outdoors. They're slim and wide, usually flipped into a triangle with a lot of different possibilities: chocolate, sugar, ice cream, Nutella, walnuts…

12. NUTELLA

Croats know foreigners love Nutella, locals love it too. We've been told it doesn't taste quite as the same as it does in their countries but generally, talking to local vendors, it's a popular choice for foreigners. A problem that often occurs here is that due to summer heat it's refrigerated and tends to be thicker than a chocolaty goodness ought to be. Local vendors serving pancakes will always have it in stock, even if they don't have other chocolate types or brands and restaurants more and more offer pancakes with Nutella as one of their dessert options.

13. ICE CREAM

Search and you will find. Split has Ice Cream on every corner and more. You can buy it in the shop; you can get scoops just about anywhere in the summer time but even in some places as the weather starts to cool, restaurants offer it on their menu for dessert whether on its own or inside pancakes. We love ice cream in all the billion types of flavors there are, some even the very odd flavors which local business now cater to.

14. BIG ON WINE

You'll quickly find that Dalmatians love alcohol. Some prefer wine, some beer, some the hard liquor so it's only natural that this affection is nurtured through good taste and a wide range of choices. Most grocery stores are heavily stocked with wine, whether it's Croatian or neighboring brands or even wines from faraway lands.

If you prefer to buy your bottles in store, you may be a bit on your own because the labels tend to be in Croatian. For example, you'll find a lot of brands from locations like Hvar, Pelješac or Istra.

Sitting in a bar or a restaurant though, you're given the possibility of talking with your waiter and finding out what they recommend, whether you prefer white, red (in Croatian, red is referred to as black) or even rosé.

15. BRANDS OF BEER

Making beer isn't Split's forte but it lacks neither Croatian nor foreign brands and is sold quite a bit. You may notice a tradition of local men buying beer in stores and sitting outside in groups during the day which is actually frowned upon but doesn't stop. Younger people purchase beer when they have no intention of spending a lot of money in clubs or simply want to hang out with their friends.

Foreign labels exist but some of the Croatian brands are: Osječko, Ožujsko, Karlovačko, Tomislav, Grička Vještica, Velebitsko.

Beer is considered the cheaper alcohol variety in comparison to wine, which is easily confirmed through its prices.

16. TRY LOCAL ALCOHOL

Just as Croats love wine and beer, we also love our local brands which to unaccustomed tasters tend to be quite hard. Dare yourself to try any type of **rakija**, a very strong fruit brandy. Basic form is colorless, with an intense smell and rough taste. Rakija is regarded as medicine (40% alcohol in general and homemade brews are even stronger). If you find that you can't possibly taste it, consider other good possibilities. Nothing brings your fever down as rakija does. It's an old wives tale (confirmed) that if you rub rakija over your back and even the soles of your feet, your fever will come down.

Rakija comes in different tastes. **Šljivovica** is produced from plums with its sweet taste which tends to trick you so you should be careful with it. **Lozovača** is made out of grapes, also quite popular for older people. Basically, any sort of fruit or mix of fruits can give a good alcohol. They're all strong and colorless unless the particular fruit gives a strong color.

17. WORLD FOOD BRANDS

Our local cuisine is rich and quite tasty; however, we do understand that not everyone is constantly open to discovering new things. Croatia, like most of the West has been heavily invaded by world food brands. So, yes, if you're craving more familiar tastes as tourists often do, you can find all the known fast foods names around Split.

Joker has only one but within City Center One and Mall of Split, the range is much bigger since both have food courts.

18. WE LOVE COFFEE

Caffeine is always great and helpful, and local population is mostly very addicted to it so it's no wonder than there is a ridiculous amount of coffee shops where it can be ordered. It's a list of common types of this heavenly nectar whether you like it black, tall, short and so on. A lot of places now offer coffee-to-go as well.

Yet again, the coffee made at home is probably tastier. Croats as a whole love coffee so much that it's very important you can buy your preferred brew in the local shops; possibly even more important.

Generally, Croats prefer what we refer to as "Turkish coffee" which is easily made and we're not big on machines as much yet. It's a simple and important thing – boil water, add sugar first and finally coffee; and it's usually made in a "đezva", a small pot with a long handle (it's more of a Turkish and Bosnian thing but it's become normal here as well). Second is the instant coffee, with many choices available, and also why private accommodation often has water heaters because why wait for the water to brew old school?

Unfortunately, this also means that I can't tell you about Starbucks because it hasn't arrived anywhere in Croatia.

Another thing that should be noted is that "having coffee" doesn't always mean going out to drink coffee. It's a term we use for meeting up with someone in a coffee shop for the sake of company and conversation. We love our coffee but it's is serious business and an important fuel, it's not meant for social sit-downs though it can be.

19. ARE YOU A SMOKER?

Smoking is still very much a thing in Croatia though newer laws have created some strict policies where it's allowed and where not (look for a label at the doors). Most coffee shops allow smoking while restaurants don't. Some will have prepared outside seating, high tables or simple ashtrays set up though this may not always be the case.

Majority of private accommodations and hotel don't allow smoking but again, either there are closed sections or an outside set up.

Prices of products are going up are nowhere near to EU prices so while locals complain, visitors mostly don't. Just remember to prepare cash because most shops won't take cards.

20. COAST LINE BEACHES

There are way too many beaches so if you know you're headed towards the Adriatic Sea; you will find at least one. From the most south areas to the furthest north, our beaches continue one after the other, interrupted only by the harbor, Riva and West Coast really, with a few more spots which would be a little hard to make use of, just about anywhere else would work to walk into and take a swim. Most popular without a doubt is Bačvice. Majority of the land just beside the sea is converted to beaches but high up in what is considered "Split 3" lays **Žnjan**. The beach is huge, primary terrain is mostly pebbles. It's become quite alive and popular in the recent years, filled with coffee shops, entertainment for children and even food.

Obojena Svjetlost (Croatian for *colored light*) is another popular choice though in the opposite direction than the aforementioned. Beauty of it is that once you've embarked on your journey that way to find a beach, there are many and it's all about what you like, nothing else. More and more our beaches are filled with coffee shops and music though not all of them so it's really about what you prefer. On this path, you'll also find other beaches, such as **Kašjuni**.

All the beaches in Split are full of sun in the best times of the years, with plenty of space. In no way does it lack what you'd need for a good time, and the newly added places add to the overall experience.

21. BAČVICE

Probably the busiest of all beaches is **Bačvice**. It's the first beach after exiting the harbor in the opposite direction from Riva and its only minutes away. Sand and a lot of sand, and by sand, I mean you will walk a long time to find something swimmable but Bačvice are busy, loud, cheerful and if you're someone who likes sand and crowds, this is where you should go.

22. BUS, TAXI, UBER

There are different ways to get around Split but it's important to remember if you're exploring Old Town, walking is the best choice.

However, if your intention is to go beyond those limits, it would be best to use one of the means of transportation: bus, taxi or Uber. Our buses often stop around the city center, at what is commonly known as "Prima" or just at the outside of our **Pazar** (green market). However, it may take a bit of maneuvering through bus numbers to figure out what you want.

Bus "3" will take you to Lora, where you will find the Poljud stadium and close to one end of Marjan, our Forest Park. Careful with **bus "5"** since its only purpose is drive up to our Municipial Court at the outskirts of Split, and doesn't drive very often. **Bus "8"** stops outside of "Pazar", which may be a good bus number because in one direction, it will lead you to "Žnjan" and in the other direction; it will lead you to "Zvončac" which is on the way between West Coast and beaches like "Obojena Svjetlost" and "Kašjuni". **Bus "12"** is a little tricky since its first and last stop is at Riva, beside Church of St. Frane but if you're looking to see "Bene", which is side of Marjan closer to Poljud. Once there, you'll find yourself enjoying a very long walk (or bike ride) but cars aren't allowed. Running is popular here.

Taxies are always waiting next to "Prima" and can be called on any of the numbers listed on the cars (it's only a few digits) and can be googled to find it for easy access. It's however important to keep in mind that our local taxies don't have too much competition yet so some may regarded as a little too expensive but they will get you where you need to go.

We also have Uber, relatively new though and not all the way too popular yet with the local population but we're certainly hearing a lot of logic why to use them.

23. RENT TRANSPORTATION

Some people prefer to rent some sort of transportation. Tourist agencies and generally a lot of places within the city center (and even the airport) offer renting cars. Cars aren't the only thing you can rent though. There are also boats, bikes and even charters.

24. WHERE TO SLEEP?

Telling you where you should rent would be rather pointless. I can tell you that more and more private accommodation is opening up and so much more space is up for rent, especially during the tourist season. To put it frank, just about everyone and their mother is getting into it so you won't be lacking options.

Hotels and hostels are available and easily found online but for cheaper renting, locals are becoming active on sites like Booking and AirBnB where location will determine how much you spend and reviews will tell you just how others felt about the place. Our most expensive rooms and apartments are within the center, especially within the Palace, but housing is generally smaller.

Renting just outside the Palace, within walking distances (ten to twenty minutes), cheaper prices and more room can be obtained. Just be sure to book earlier because our tourist counts are growing with each year.

25. CAMPING

Split can offer you camping as well, closest one being furthest south of the city, in **Stobreč**. Alternatively, you could find the campsite **Slatine**, located on a small island Čiovo (connected to the smaller city Trogir with a bridge). First one may be closer than the other and Čiovo's problem during the summer is the single connecting bridge making for a lot of traffic jams but each will give you the camping benefits.

26. THEATRES

Age of cinema has certainly played its part with theatres. There was a time when there were a number of local cinemas, all within Old Town, where we could watch movies but their age has since lost passed so many of them have been reworked (like cinema Central is now a club or cinema Karaman is a bar/restaurant). Our theatres are few but still strive.

Croatian National Theatre in Split deserves first mention. Even if you're not the theatre type, the outside of the building is beautiful and the inside is breathtaking just as a beautiful old theatre house ought to be. It's housed near "Prima" so be sure to check it out. It's has its own website so be sure to look up "HNK Split" if you're curious in attending a performance.

City Youth Theatre is located in the same building where cinema Karaman once resided. It's more focused on youth same as is the **City Doll Theatre**.

Be warned however, other than the foreign visits into the Croatian National Theatre, our Theatres really do most of its work in Croatian so it may not be suitable for foreigners but if you're interested in learning, it can be an adventure.

27. ENJOY OUR HISTORY

Ten. That is the number of museums you can visit while visiting Split. If you're not planning on spending too much time in our fair city, you should probably think about what would interest you the most but if you're planning on staying a little longer then you should probably just go for all of them.

Some of those are: Archeological museum, Natural History Museum, Split City Museum, Split Hall of Fame, Museum of Croatian Archeological Statues in Split and even the Live Museum. Each houses its unique setting.

28. ARE YOU AN ART LOVER?

There are fourteen galleries throughout Split. Some of these will house different exhibitions depending on what is visiting or possibly house other events like lectures while others are extremely focused on particular artists.

For example, galleries devoted to particular artists are the Vidović Gallery, University Gallery "Vlasko Lipovac" who's Studio you could also see at a different location and Meštrović Gallery. Each of these artists have left remarkable work behind, first two being painters and the last one a sculpture. Be sure to check them out.

Galleries that house different exhibitions are the substructure of the Palace, Salon Galić, Art Gallery, Coservation Department Gallery, Croatian-French Society, Gallery Morska, Kula Gallery, Jakšić Gallery and others.

Split is big on art. We like to hold exhibitions and we like to praise those who have left a powerful impact on the country and the city. If you love art, you'll enjoy visiting these places.

29. OUR MUSIC

Our three famous composers are Josip Hatze, Ivan Tijardović and Zdenko Runjić. Hatze composed music, including music for our poetry writer Vladimir Nazor (mandatory material for all Croatian children); Tijardović created Operettas, Musicals and Operas and if you get a chance to see his work, you absolutely should. Runjić was a songwriter who created close to 700 songs and has collaborated with some very notable artists, some who are still active today. He even founded the Melodies of Croatian Adriatic.

30. SINGERS AND BANDS

Oliver Dragojević, Gibonni, Severina, Dino Dvornik, Jasmin Stavros, Neno Belan, Goran Karan, Dražen Zečić, Doris Dragović, Jelena Rozga, Siniša Vuco and Meri Cetinić. These are our famous singers. Majority of them are still active today, in 2017, and work of all of them can be today found online. Their melody is beautiful and words are often powerful to affect the soul. Our groups included Daleka Obala, Magazin and Tutti Frutti.

The work of all our artists is mostly in Croatian, with the occasional flirtation with English or Italian and collaborations with foreign artists. You should still check out their music and maybe translate some of the words if you particularly like them. And if you're lucky, you might come to Split when any of our artists are performing or hear even more during festivals.

31. LIVE MUSIC AND DJS

For many years, we've had yearly festivals to which locals often flocked to. Many of our musicians partake and it also serves to give a chance to unknown artists. Our music festivals take place during the summer and often staged on **Prokurative**.

During the summer there will often be live music and DJs playing all around different locations. Not all of them will however be too advertised so the best advice I could give you is while you're in the city, follow either the music or the lights aimed at the sky (outdoor bars often have them). Also, near the Golden Gate, live music from local and unknown artists is becoming popular though they tend to not last long into the night due to the residents.

Summer time is full of music. DJs will play in bars and clubs in the evenings but day bars on the beaches will often have DJs to make the beach experience all the more interesting.

All music has a limit though so don't be surprised when it's cut off at certain times in the night. Residents tend to have different arrangements. Park music may end earlier than outdoor bars (some have to go quiet by no later than two am, some even sooner) while clubs tend to stay open and play music to at least four or five am, sometimes even to the early morning (like the club at beach Bačvice).

32. ULTRA MUSIC FESTIVAL

For several years now, Split has been host to the **Ultra Music Festival**, "Europe's infamous electronic music festival" as their own website describes it. It takes place during the summer, taking over our **Poljud stadium**, for no more than three nights. If this is your thing, be sure to book accommodation early due to the increase in prices.

33. "THE SPORTIEST CITY IN THE WORLD"

The second largest city of Croatia also likes to pride itself in being "the sportiest city in the world" since we make room for soccer, tennis, basketball, swimming, rowing, sailing, waterpolo, athletics and handball. Everyone has their thing but probably the loudest are the soccer fans. **Poljud Stadium** is where all the games are played, our club is Hajduk and their fans are Torcida Split.

Because of our love to sports, Split has given a lot of famous players in different sports with names such as Slaven Billić, Igor Tudor and Stipe Pletikosić (soccer); Toni Kukoč and Dino Rađa (basketball); Goran Ivanišević, Wimbledon champion in 2001 and Mario Ančić (tennis). Our rowing club has a lot of medals, swimming has a long tradition. Blanka Vlašić is our famous athlete.

Split has hosted many sports events such as the 1979 Mediterranean Games, 1990 European Athletics Championships and most recently, the 2009 World Men's Handball Championship (alongside other Croatian cities) for which the **Spaladium Arena** was built not too far from Poljud Stadium. Both places will be the main attraction for games but also music concerts when necessary.

34. HOW SHOULD YOU SEE THE CITY?

There are a lot of ways how you could see the city. Obvious answer, especially for the city center would be walking because it's absolutely the best way to see the city. If you're looking for other sights, there's of course the bus, taxi, Uber or renting.

Take a bike ride throughout the city and see plenty that way or go rock climbing and get a whole different view… there's really a lot of different ways and Split is well aware of what it has to offer.

35. BUY AT "PAZAR"

You will probably more than once hear the word **Pazar** during your stay. This is our green market, laid out between the harbor and Riva. Life there starts early and often dies out drastically by late noon or soon after. During the busy times, you can buy food such vegetables, fruits, meat etc. Second area of the market tends to be used for selling used things and cheaper clothes and accessories can be bought. This latter areas work longer.

36. SHOPPING

Split has no shortage of shopping. We have three shopping malls located in the city or its outskirts. In Old Town, you can find **Prima**, while a little further away are **Joker** and **Prima 3**, while **Mall of Split** can be found on the exit leading towards Solin and Dugopolje whereas **City Centar One** is on the path further down south.

In our shopping malls you can find what you may need like food, medicine, cosmetics, famous clothing brands and the occasional local brands and a whole of other things (including movies).

In the city center is where local small shops are but there are still plenty of options there like trinkets, tourist oriented shops, clothing and shoe brands, especially more local ones and even more focused shops such as ones that sell Game of Thrones and other famous memorabilia.

37. LIFE IN THE CENTER

Majority of our city life takes place in the center of the city, which is the Palace and nearby. Majority of what you may need can be found there: restaurants, coffee shops, stores, small shops, fast foods, and a lot of space gets rented out by tourists...

It's only with the building of the shopping malls that people have shifted to visiting them, having their coffee there and shopping. Bad weather tends to take locals to the malls quite a bit.

38. TAKE A STROLL THROUGH OUR PARKS

Green areas are well tended to and busy. In the summer, they will even be occupied by live music playing. Four parks stand out.

Sustipan comes after you've walked through the West Coast and offers tranquility and a beautiful view. Interesting tidbit about the location is that it was once the final resting place for Croatian Kings and later the first city cemetery though it was torn down decades ago to make it the beautiful park it is today. Don't be surprised if you spot the occasional bride and groom taking wedding photographs there!

Park of Strossmayer is commonly referred to as "Đardin" by locals, located right outside the Golden Gate and the Statue of Grgur Ninski. This is where you will find local artists performing in the summer, with improvised vendors serving alcoholic and non-alcoholic beverages during the events and antique stands at the edges where you can purchase old silverware, vinyl and home trinkets.

Park of Emanuel Vidović is far from either location. Once more, Split has chosen to honor its famous painter by naming one of its beautiful parks after him. Nearby are schools though so young people tend to circulate it.

Katalinić hill (**Katalinića brig**) is located between the harbor and beach Bačvice, with its primary purpose as the location of St. Peter de Buctis Church and later served as a defense fort for attacks from the Sea and as many of our locations, offers a great view.

39. WE HAVE A VOLCANO

Marjan is commonly referred to as the Park Forest but a little more interesting tidbit is that it is actually a quiet volcano. It won't erupt, we promise! Instead, it's a very popular green area of our city, a little secluded but still easily accessible from different areas. Marjan offers a number of different activities and beautiful locations to see. It's often used by walkers, families wanting to enjoy picnics, by cyclists and hikers. Dog walkers take their dog there and runners take long runs.

There are a number of ways to get there and a number of different outlooks. From Riva, nearest you can find are the walking grounds and the forest. Walking grounds are open to the cost while the forest offers that more green setting and is essentially a series of stairs leading up to the area where families gather and events are often held (such as our Labor day event on May 1st where by a long standing tradition, cooked beans are handed out to citizens) though the area offers a good walk and playgrounds for children.

The alternative are **Bene** which are the opposite side of the Park forest, a road closed off from driving which is particularly used by athletes, cyclists and families taking their children to area where children play, families enjoy the Sea or sit at the coffee shop and on events even enjoy pony rides.

This is still a forest though, so there is no reason to be lost here in the dark or without company.

40. CITY OF DOG LOVERS

We love our dogs, sometimes even a little too much so we like to spoil them rotten. Pet stores are all around with helpful service. Dog parks aren't quite as common. Split is home to the official walking grounds for dogs and **Duilovo**, dog beach. And some closed dog areas.

We're also not always law abiding so you may see free dogs in parks that don't allow them. Fines tend to not scare local people too much so if you're a proud puppy mom or dad, Split is quite open to animals.

41. PARKING PROBLEMS

Driving and parking in the strictest center of the town is forbidden unless one has a special permission (reserved for residents). Recently, more and more people have been disregarding this and slide through but you should keep in mind that police could be lurking and your car could be picked up if parked in the forbidden area.

There are parking sections which charge exit as well as spots marked where you can pay for an hour or two with your phone or the nearby machine.

Free parking is a particular pet peeve for us, especially for people who live just outside those strict center lines where buildings are surrounded with parking meant for residents but are often occupied by people who either live further away or in the nearby cities which takes away our space. We don't mind guests who are staying in private accommodation but visitors (local too) tend to take up space so all we ask is that you be considerate to the locals and pay for parking where parking should be paid rather than having problems.

Another important thing to remember when finding parking in the city is that if you fail to follow the rules, our car pickers, which we call **"Pauk služba"**, are merciless in collecting cars. Whether local or foreign license plates, they will pick up just about anyone and the fines aren't worth the trouble. They often won't even consider removing the tire plate once it's been placed so always be careful how you park in Split. Primarily, never block out any of the trash containers, take even an inch of an invalid parking space and don't leave your car in space not marked for parking. Locals are guilty of the last but they do it at their own risk so don't be like them, the fine isn't worth it.

42. GAME OF THRONES

As many fans of the show know, many scenes of the hit TV series Game of Thrones were filmed in Croatia. A lot of this filming was done in Dubrovnik, but Split received its fifteen minutes of fame too. Locations throughout the Diocletian's Palace were used; especially its basements along with the out of town Klis Fortress. Even though these are no longer active film locations, you can find organized tours.

Fans can also find several stores selling TV show memorabilia. Simply search "Game of Thrones Split shops" to find their exact locations, one of which offers a lot of different memorabilia (such as Star Wars, Harry Potter, Marvel and so much more). I can promise you that for a fan, these shops are absolutely worth a visit and the products are quite diverse.

43. OUTSIDE THE CITY

Lot of things happens in the city though it may not seem like it when you first take glance. One should never leave Split without at least checking the ruins of Salona. In this case, joining an organized tour so a guide can give you a better idea of its history and layout may be a good idea.

Secondly, if you like shopping, **Dugopolje** is a small city not too far from Split (also our main access to the highway) which offers Outlet shopping.

The closest mountain to Split is **Kozjak**, big and tough but if you're a hiker or interested in its natural beauty, you should check out our local hiking groups based in Split (and get professional guides!).

44. LOCAL ISLANDS

There are over a thousand islands in the entirety of our country but nearest to city, you will find Hvar, Šolta and Brač, our pride and joys because of which, ferries and fast boats are always available. Our ferry company is called Jadrolinija and its ticket booths and offices can be found all through the main harbor (also our train and bus stations).

Why should you visit any of these islands? First and foremost: beautiful beaches everywhere. On each of the islands you will find good wine and rich olive oil straight from the growers (often best to check local markets).

Hvar is our sunniest island which offers plenty in regards to history, entertainment, beauty and tasting purposes. Ferry takes about two hours to reach its harbor from which you can either take one of the buses to visit towns or drive. Alternatively, you could take one of the fast boats straight to one of its cities. Lavender is very popular and heavily grown so there is no shortage of products. In the summer, the night life is quite alive as well.

Ferry ride to **Brač** takes about fifty minutes. They too strive on tourism but also fishing and agriculture. Their precious white stone is an object of pride, which was used in building the Diocletian's Palace and the Canadian National Vimy Memorial. They will also proudly claim the White House in the US was built with it but we can neither confirm nor deny this.

Šolta is much smaller in size and the journey there is a lot shorter but wine, olive and beaches are great there as well.

45. EXCURSIONS

Another important fact about Split is that it's often used as a base for our visitors. Our tourist agencies are well aware of this so the possibility of organized excursions to either one of our islands (sometimes specific locations even) or any of the near towns, rivers or lakes. From Split, you can enjoy a day at Plitvice lakes (one of Croatia's many national parks), enjoy swimming at the Krka waterfalls, visit Bosnia's Mostar and so much more, all done in package deals with different prices.

46. OLIVE PICKING

Dalmatians are big on making olive oil, so much so that throughout the region and islands, you will find a lot of oil plantations. This is a hard but overall rewarding work for our growers and a growing attraction for tourists. Year 2017 marked the First World Competition in olive picking on Hvar where people from different counties were able to compete (Italy, Montenegro, Hungary, New Zeeland and much more). If you'd love to try your hand at the experience, local growers are more and more looking for help and organizing excursions.

47. SOME LOCAL PHRASES

Croatians vary in foreign languages. English is a fast growing necessity in the city but many of the people spent their educations learning other languages (either alongside English or without it). Locals can sometimes be better at Italian or even German but of course, Croatian is our first language. Our grammar is hard to some but we'll appreciate the effort.

For example, for your basic greeting you can use: **Dobar dan** (good day), **dobro jutro** (good morning), **dobra večer** (good evening), **doviđenja** (goodbye), **bok** (bye).

Our etiquette words would be as follows: **hvala** (thank you), **puno hvala** (thank you very much), **molim Vas** (respectful please where *Vas* is used to address a person you don't know, especially someone older) or **molim te** (please used with our friends and people on first name basis), **nema na čemu** (you're welcome), **oprostite / oprosti** (Pardon or even an apology, first one being the more polite and the second one more informal and personal).

These phrases are probably the most basic ones but if you'd like some little more help a visitor you can use any of the following: **Možete li mi pomoći?** (Can you help me?) or **Gdje je...** (Where is...?).

48. IMPORTANT TO REMEMBER

The currency is **Croatian kuna (HRK)** and while we are part of the European Union and Euro is more and more accepted as a possible alternative, we're far from actively using it in commerce so it would be best for you to change your money when you arrive. Alternatively, you can use different cards.

If you need any sort of help in Croatia, all our services use three digit phone numbers that can easily be found online. There is also a primary number which will connect you to the department you may need (police, firefighters, hospital, national search and rescue at sea).

Split has two hospitals and a lot of general practice doctors. Hospitals are called **Firule** and **Križine**, they're not far from each other. Main road that leads to both starts off from the harbor and isn't too far away. Different departments are in different hospitals but there's an ER in each.

49. LAST MINUTE ADVICE

Split is a big city in Croatian terms though it obviously lacks in size to some worldly cities such as New York, Rome or Sydney. It's even quite smaller than our capital Zagreb and yet the second in size in Croatia. We're friendly people and relaxed but life in the city takes its toll on people and we tend to be busy and rushed sometimes. Try not to hold it against us. Mind the driving as well because some our intersections may be small but are still quite dangerous.

The city may not be to everyone's taste but it's certainly a place you should visit more than once because not even all locals have explored every part of it or been to every restaurant, coffee shop or club. It's ever growing and changing so if you've liked us once, by all means come again! You'll find new places and new experiences each time you do.

50. INFORMATION ONLINE

Finally, I'd like to remind you that the internet is your friend and should be taken as such. Online, you can find what you're looking for. Information for visitors is very detailed and often in English so you can trust to find what you're looking for.

We have tourist boards and guide websites which offer a lot of information but also separate information that can be found through the search engine. You should especially look into review sites such as Foursquare and different review sites online. Croats are still growing to use them but other visitors are very immaculate and honest in using them so you can quickly find whether you've discovered a good place to eat or drink coffee at, find shops and events.

TOP REASONS TO BOOK THIS TRIP

History: Our beautiful and long history is celebrated and eagerly shared with others. Whether you're a fan of stories or the architecture, you won't be disappointed.

Mediterranean food: We may be easy to take what others offer us and bring it into our city, but our own cuisine never lacks and shouldn't be missed out on.

Beaches: Split a city built on the very coast of the Adriatic Sea so you will find many different beaches and scenes for you to enjoy, whatever your preference may be.

Wine: Where we lack in beer making, we make up for it in a plethora of fine wines of all colors. You should absolutely try our local brands!

Bonus Book

50 THINGS TO KNOW ABOUT PACKING LIGHT FOR TRAVEL

Pack the Right Way Every Time

Author: Manidipa Bhattacharyya

First Published in 2015 by Dr. Lisa Rusczyk. Copyright 2015. All Rights Reserved. No part of this publication may be reproduced, including scanning and photocopying, or distributed in any form or by any means, electronic or mechanical, or stored in a database or retrieval system without prior written permission from the publisher.

Disclaimer: The publisher has put forth an effort in preparing and arranging this book. The information provided herein by the author is provided "as is". Use this information at your own risk. The publisher is not a licensed doctor. Consult your doctor before engaging in any medical activities. The publisher and author disclaim any liabilities for any loss of profit or commercial or personal damages resulting from the information contained in this book.

Edited by Melanie Howthorne

Introduction

*He who would travel happily
must travel light.*

-Antoine de Saint-Exupéry

Travel takes you to different places from seas and mountains to deserts and much more. In your travels you get to interact with different people and their cultures. You will, however, enjoy the sights and interact positively with these new people even more, if you are travelling light.

When you travel light your mind can be free from worry about your belongings. You do not have to spend precious vacation time waiting for your luggage to arrive after a long flight. There is be no chance of your bags going missing and the best part is that you need not pay a fee for checked baggage.

People who have mastered this art of packing light will root for you to take only one carry-on, wherever you go. However, many people can find it really hard to pack light. More so if you are travelling with children. Differentiating between "must have" and "just in case" items is the starting point. There will be ample shopping avenues at your destination which are just waiting to be explored.

This book will show you 'packing' in a new 'light' – pun intended – and help you to embrace light packing practices for all of your future travels.

Off to packing!

Dedication

I dedicate this book to all the travel buffs that I know, who have given me great insights into the contents of their backpacks.

About The Author

Manidipa Bhattacharyya is a creative writer and editor, with an education in English literature and Linguistics. After working in the IT industry for seven long years she decided to call it quits and follow her heart instead. Manidipa has been ghost writing, editing, proof reading and doing secondary research services for many story tellers and article writers for about three years. She stays in Kolkata, India with her husband and a busy two year old. In her own time Manidipa enjoys travelling, photography and writing flash fiction.

Manidipa believes in travelling light and never carries anything that she couldn't haul herself on a trip. However, travelling with her child changed the scenario. She seemed to carry the entire world with her for the baby on the first two trips. But good sense prevailed and she is again working her way to becoming a light traveler, this time with a kid.

The Right Travel Gear

1. Choose Your Travel Gear Carefully

While selecting your travel gear, pick items that are light weight, durable and most importantly, easy to carry. There are cases with wheels so you can drag them along – these are usually on the heavy side because of the trolley. Alternatively a backpack that you can carry comfortably on your back, or even a duffel bag that you can carry easily by hand or sling across your body are also great options. Whatever you choose, one thing to keep in mind is that the luggage itself should not weigh a ton, this will give you the flexibility to bring along one extra pair of shoes if you so desire.

2. Carry The Minimum Number Of Bags

Selecting light weight luggage is not everything. You need to restrict the number of bags you carry as well. One carry-on size bag is ideal for light travel. Most carriers allow one cabin baggage plus one purse, handbag or camera bag as long as it slides under the seat in front. So technically, you can carry two items of luggage without checking them in.

3. Pack One Extra Bag

Always pack one extra empty bag along with your essential items. This could be a very light weight duffel bag or even a sturdy tote bag which takes up minimal space. In the event that you end up buying a lot of souvenirs, you already have a handy bag to stuff all that into and do not have to spend time hunting for an appropriate bag.

> *I'm very strict with my packing and have everything in its right place. I never change a rule. I hardly use anything in the hotel room. I wheel my own wardrobe in and that's it.*
>
> Charlie Watts

Clothes & Accessories

4. Plan Ahead

Figure out in advance what you plan to do on your trip. That will help you to pick that one dress you need for the occasion. If you are going to attend a wedding then you have to carry formal wear. If not, you can ditch the gown for something lighter that will be comfortable during long walks or on the beach.

5. Wear That Jacket

Remember that wearing items will not add extra luggage for your air travel. So wear that bulky jacket that you plan to carry for your trip. This saves space and can also help keep you warm during the chilly flight.

6. Mix and Match

Carry clothes that can be interchangeably used to reinvent your look. Find one top that goes well with a couple of pairs of pants or skirts. Use tops, shirts and jackets wisely along with other accessories like a scarf or a stole to create a new look.

7. Choose Your Fabric Wisely

Stuffing clothes in cramped bags definitely takes its toll which results in wrinkles. It is best to carry wrinkle free, synthetic clothes or merino tops. This will eliminate the need for that small iron you usually bring along.

8. Ditch Clothes Pack Underwear

Pack more underwear and socks. These are the things that will give you a fresh feel even if you do not get a chance to wear fresh clothes. Moreover these are easy to wash and can be dried inside the hotel room itself.

9. Choose Dark Over Light

While picking your clothes choose dark coloured ones. They are easy to colour coordinate and can last longer before needing a wash. Accidental food spills and dirt from the road are less visible on darker clothes.

10. Wear Your Jeans

Take only one pair of Jeans with you, which you should wear on the flight. Remember to pick a pair that can be worn for sightseeing trips and is equally eloquent for dinner. You can add variety by adding light weight cargoes and chinos.

11. Carry Smart Accessories

The right accessory can give you a fresh look even with the same old dress. An intelligent neck-piece, a couple of bright scarves, stoles or a sarong can be used in a number of ways to add variety to your clothing. These light weight beauties can double up as a nursing cover, a light blanket, beach wear, a modesty cover for visiting places of worship, and also makes for an enthralling game of peek-a-boo.

12. Learn To Fold Your Garments

Seasoned travellers all swear by rolling their clothes for compact and wrinkle free packing. Bundle packing, where you roll the clothes around a central object as if tying it up, is also a popular method of compact and wrinkle free packing. Stacking folded clothes one on top of another is a big no-no as it makes creases extreme and they are difficult to get rid of without ironing.

13. Wash Your Dirty Laundry

One of the ways to avoid carrying loads of clothes is to wash the clothes you carry. At some places you might get to use the laundry services or a Laundromat but if you are in a pinch, best solution is to wash them yourself. If that is the plan then carrying quick drying clothes is highly recommended, which most often also happen to be the wrinkle free variety.

14. Leave Those Towels Behind

Regular towels take up a lot of space, are heavy and take ages to dry out. If you are staying at hotels they will provide you with towels anyway. If you are travelling to a remote place, where the availability of towels look doubtful, carry a light weight travel towel of viscose material to do the job.

15. Use A Compression Bag

Compression bags are getting lots of recommendation now days from regular travellers. These are useful for saving space in your luggage when you have to pack bulky dresses. While packing for the return trip, get help from the hotel staff to arrange a vacuum cleaner.

Footwear

16. Put On Your Hiking Boots

If you have plans to go hiking or trekking during your trip, you will need those bulky hiking boots. The best way to carry them is to wear them on flight to save space and luggage weight. You can remove the boots once inside and be comfortable in your socks.

17. Picking The Right Shoes

Shoes are often the bulkiest items, along with being the dainty if you are a female. They need care and take up a lot of space in your luggage. It is advisable therefore to pick shoes very carefully. If you plan to do a lot of walking and site seeing, then wearing a pair of comfortable walking shoes are a must. For more formal occasions you can carry durable, light weight flats which will not take up much space.

18. Stuff Shoes

If you happen to pack a pair of shoes, ensure you utilize their hollow insides. Tuck small items like rolled up socks or belts to save space. They will also be easy to find.

Toiletries
19. Stashing Toiletries

Carry only absolute necessities. Airline rules dictate that for one carry-on bag, liquids and gels must be in 3.4 ounce (100ml) bottles or less, and must be packed in a one quart zip-lock bag. If you are planning to stay in a hotel, the basic things will be provided for you. It's best is to buy the rest from the local market at your destination.

20. Take Along Tampons

Tampons are a hard to find item in a lot of countries. Figure out how many you need and pack accordingly. For longer stays you can buy them online and have them delivered to where you are staying.

21. Get Pampered Before You Travel

Some avid travellers suggest getting a pedicure and manicure just the day before travelling. This not only gives you a well kept look, you also save the trouble of packing nail polish. Remember, every little bit of weight reduced adds up.

Electronics
22. Lugging Along Electronics

Electronics have a large role to play in our lives today. Most of us cannot imagine our lives away from our phones, laptops or tablets. However while travelling, one must consider the amount of weight these electronics add to our luggage. Thankfully smart phones come along with all the essentials tools like a camera, email access, picture editing tools and more. They are smart to the point of eliminating the need to carry multiple gadgets. Choose a smart phone that suits all your requirements and travel with the world in your palms or pocket.

23. Reduce the Number of Chargers

If you do travel with multiple electronic devices, you will have to bear the additional burden of carrying all their chargers too. Check if a single charger can be used for multiple devices. You might also consider investing in a pocket charger. These small devices support multiple devices while keeping you charged on the go.

24. Travel Friendly Apps

Along with smart phones come numerous apps, which are immensely helpful in our travels. You name it and you have an app for it at hand – take pictures, sharing with friends and family, torch to light dark roads, maps, checking flight/train times, find hotels and many other things. Use these smart alternatives to traditional items like books to eliminate weight and save space.

> *I get ideas about what's essential when packing my suitcase.*
>
> -Diane von Furstenberg

Travelling With Kids

25. Bring Along the Stroller

Kids might enjoy walking for a while but they soon tire out and a stroller is the just the right thing for them to rest in while you continue your tour. Strollers also double duty as a luggage carrier and shopping bag holder. Remember to pick a light weight, easy to handle brand of stroller. Better yet, find out in advance if you can rent a stroller at your destination.

26. Bring Only Enough Diapers for Your Trip

Diapers take up a lot of space and add to the weight of your luggage. Therefore it is advisable to carry just enough diapers to last through the trip and a few for afterwards, till you buy fresh stock at your destination. Unless of course you are travelling to a really remote area, in which case you have no choice but to carry the load. Otherwise diapers are something you will find pretty easily.

27. Take Only A Couple Of Toys

Children are easily attracted by new things in their environment. While travelling they will find numerous 'new' objects to scrutinize and play with. Packing just one favorite toy is enough, or if there is no favorite toy leave out all of them in favor of stories or imaginary games.

28. Carry Kid Friendly Snacks

Create a small snack counter in your bag to store away quick bites for those sudden hunger pangs. Depending on the child's age this could include chocolates, raisins, dry fruits, granola bars or biscuits. Also keep a bottle of water handy for your little one. These things do not add much weight and can be adjusted in a handbag or knapsack.

29. Games to Carry

Create some travel specific, imaginary games if you have slightly grown up children, like spot the attractions. Keep a coloring book and colors handy for in-flight or hotel time. Apps on your smart phone can keep the children engaged with cartoons and story books. Older children are often entertained by games available on phones or tablets. This cuts the weight of luggage down while keeping the kids entertained.

30. Let the Kids Carry Their Load

A good thing is to start early sharing of responsibilities. Let your child pick a bag of his or her choice and pack it themselves. Keep tabs on what they are stuffing in their bags by asking if they will be using that item on the trip. It could start out being just an entertainment bag initially but with growing years they will learn to sort the useful from the superfluous. Children as little as four can maneuver a small trolley suitcase like a pro- their experience in pull along toys credit. If you are worried that you may be pulling it for them, you may want to start with a backpack.

31. Decide on Location for Children to Sleep

While on a trip you might not always get a crib at your destination, and carrying one will make life all the more difficult. Instead call ahead to see if there are any cribs or roll out beds for children. You may even put blankets on the floor. Weave them a story about camping and they will gladly sleep without any trouble.

32. Get Baby Products Delivered At Your Destination

If you are absolutely paranoid about not getting your favourite variety of diaper or brand of baby food, check out online stores like amazon.com for services in your destination city. You can buy things online ahead of your travel and get them delivered to your hotel upon arrival.

33. Feeding Needs Of Your Infants

If you are travelling with a breastfed infant, you save the trouble of carrying bottles and bottle sanitization kits. For special food, or medications, you may need to call ahead to make sure you have a refrigerator where you are staying.

34. Feeding Needs of Your Toddler

With the progression from infancy to toddler, their dietary requirements too evolve. You will have to pack some snacks for travelling time. Fresh fruits and vegetables can be purchased at your destination. Most of the cities you travel to in whichever part of the world, will have baby food products and formulas, available at the local drug-store or the supermarket.

35. Picking Clothes for Your Baby

Contrary to popular belief, babies can do without many changes of clothes. At the most pack 2 outfits per day. Pack mix and match type clothes for your little one as well. Pick things which are comfortable to wear and quick to dry.

36. Selecting Shoes for Your Baby

Like outfits, kids can make do with two pairs of comfortable shoes. If you can get some water resistant shoes it will be best. To expedite drying wet shoes, you can stuff newspaper in them then wrap them with newspaper and leave them to dry overnight.

37. Keep One Change of Clothes Handy

Travelling with kids can be tricky. Keep a change of clothes for the kids and mum handy in your purse or tote bag. This takes a bit of space in your hand luggage but comes extremely handy in case there are any accidents or spills.

38. Leave Behind Baby Accessories

Baby accessories like their bed, bath tub, car seat, crib etc. should be left at home. Many hotels provide a crib on request, while car seats can be borrowed from friends or rented. Babies can be given a bath in the hotel sink or even in the adult bath tub with a little bit of water. If you bring a few bath toys, they can be used in the bath, pool, and out of water. They can also be sanitized easily in the sink.

39. Carry a Small Load Of Plastic Bags

With children around there are chances of a number of soiled clothes and diapers. These plastic bags help to sort the dirt from the clean inside your big bag. These are very light weight and come in handy to other carry stuff as well at times.

Pack with a Purpose

40. Packing for Business Trips

One neutral-colored suit should suffice. It can be paired with different shirts, ties and accessories for different occasions. One pair of black suit pants could be worn with a matching jacket for the office or with a snazzy top for dinner.

41. Packing for A Cruise

Most cruises have formal dinners, and that formal dress usually takes up a lot of space. However you might find a tuxedo to rent. For women, a short black dress with multiple accessory options will do the trick.

42. Packing for A Long Trip Over Different Climates

The secret packing mantra for travel over multiple climates is layering. Layering traps air around your body creating insulation against the cold. The same light t-shirt that is comfortable in a warmer climate can be the innermost layer in a colder climate.

Reduce Some More Weight

43. Leave Precious Things At Home

Things that you would hate to lose or get damaged leave them at home. Precious jewelry, expensive gadgets or dresses, could be anything. You will not require these on your trip. Leave them at home and spare the load on your mind.

44. Send Souvenirs by Mail

If you have spent all your money on purchasing souvenirs, carrying them back in the same bag that you brought along would be difficult. Either pack everything in another bag and check it in the airport or get everything shipped to your home. Use an international carrier for a secure transit, but this could be more expensive than the checking fees at the airport.

45. Avoid Carrying Books

Books equal to weight. There are many reading apps which you can download on your smart phone or tab. Plus there are gadgets like Kindle and Nook that are thinner and lighter alternatives to your regular book.

Check, Get, Set, Check Again

46. Strategize Before Packing

Create a travel list and prepare all that you think you need to carry along. Keep everything on your bed or floor before packing and then think through once again – do I really need that? Any item that meets this question can be avoided. Remove whatever you don't really need and pack the rest.

47. Test Your Luggage

Once you have fully packed for the trip take a test trip with your luggage. Take your bags and go to town for window shopping for an hour. If you enjoy your hour long trip it is good to go, if not, go home and reduce the load some more. Repeat this test till you hit the right weight.

48. Add a Roll Of Duct Tape

You might wonder why, when this book has been talking about reducing stuff, we're suddenly asking you to pack something totally unusual. This is because when you have limited supplies, duct tape is immensely helpful for small repairs – a broken bag, leaking zip-lock bag, broken sunglasses, you name it and duct tape can fix it, temporarily.

49. List of Essential Items

Even though the emphasis is on packing light, there are things which have to be carried for any trip. Here is our list of essentials:

- Passport/Visa or any other ID

- Any other paper work that might be required on a trip like permits, hotel reservation confirmations etc.

- Medicines – all your prescription medicines and emergency kit, especially if you are travelling with children

- Medical or vaccination records

- Money in foreign currency if travelling to a different country

- Tickets- Email or Message them to your phone

50. Make the Most of Your Trip

Wherever you are going, whatever you hope to do we encourage you to embrace it whole-heartedly. Take in the scenery, the culture and above all, enjoy your time away from home.

On a long journey even a straw weighs heavy.

-Spanish Proverb

Packing and Planning Tips

A Week before Leaving

- Arrange for someone to take care of pets and water plants
- Stop mail and newspaper
- Notify Credit Card companies where you are going.
- Change your thermostat settings
- Car inspected, oil is changed, and tires have the correct pressure.
- Passports and id is up to date.
- Pay bills.
- Copy important items and download travel Apps.
- Start collecting small bills for tips

Right Before Leaving

- Clean out refrigerator.
- Empty garbage cans.
- Lock windows.
- Make sure you have the right ID with you.
- Bring cash for tips.
- Remember travel documents.
- Lock door behind you.
- Remember wallet.
- Unplug items in house and pack chargers.

Read other Greater Than a Tourist Books

Greater Than a Tourist San Miguel de Allende Guanajuato Mexico:
50 Travel Tips from a Local by Tom Peterson

Greater Than a Tourist – Lake George Area New York USA:
50 Travel Tips from a Local by Janine Hirschklau

Greater Than a Tourist – Monterey California United States:
50 Travel Tips from a Local by Katie Begley

Greater Than a Tourist – Chanai Crete Greece:
50 Travel Tips from a Local by Dimitra Papagrigoraki

Greater Than a Tourist – The Garden Route Western Cape Province South Africa:
50 Travel Tips from a Local by Li-Anne McGregor van Aardt

Greater Than a Tourist – Sevilla Andalusia Spain:
50 Travel Tips from a Local by Gabi Gazon

Greater Than a Tourist – Kota Bharu Kelantan Malaysia:
50 Travel Tips from a Local by Aditi Shukla

Children's Book: Charlie the Cavalier Travels the World by Lisa Rusczyk

> TOURIST

Visit Greater Than a Tourist for Free Travel Tips
  http://GreaterThanATourist.com

Sign up for the Greater Than a Tourist Newsletter for discount days, new books, and travel information:
  http://eepurl.com/cxspyf

Follow us on Facebook for tips, images, and ideas:
  https://www.facebook.com/GreaterThanATourist

Follow us on Pinterest for travel tips and ideas:
  http://pinterest.com/GreaterThanATourist

Follow us on Instagram for beautiful travel images:
  http://Instagram.com/GreaterThanATourist

> TOURIST

Please leave your honest review of this book on Amazon and Goodreads. Please send your feedback to GreaterThanaTourist@gmail.com as we continue to improve the series. Thank you. We appreciate your positive and constructive feedback. Thank you.

METRIC CONVERSIONS

TEMPERATURE

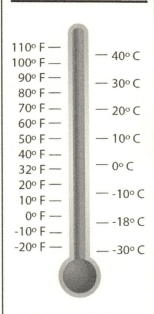

110° F — 40° C
100° F
90° F — 30° C
80° F
70° F — 20° C
60° F
50° F — 10° C
40° F
32° F — 0° C
20° F
10° F — -10° C
0° F — -18° C
-10° F
-20° F — -30° C

To convert F to C:
Subtract 32, and then multiply by 5/9 or .5555.

To Convert C to F:
Multiply by 1.8 and then add 32.

32F = 0C

LIQUID VOLUME

To Convert:	Multiply by
U.S. Gallons to Liters	3.8
U.S. Liters to Gallons	.26
Imperial Gallons to U.S. Gallons	1.2
Imperial Gallons to Liters	4.55
Liters to Imperial Gallons	.22

1 Liter = .26 U.S. Gallon
1 U.S. Gallon = 3.8 Liters

DISTANCE

To convert	Multiply by
Inches to Centimeters	2.54
Centimeters to Inches	.39
Feet to Meters	.3
Meters to Feet	3.28
Yards to Meters	.91
Meters to Yards	1.09
Miles to Kilometers	1.61
Kilometers to Miles	.62

1 Mile = 1.6 km
1 km = .62 Miles

WEIGHT

1 Ounce = .28 Grams
1 Pound = .4555 Kilograms
1 Gram = .04 Ounce
1 Kilogram = 2.2 Pounds

TRAVEL QUESTIONS

- Do you bring presents home to family or friends after a vacation?
- Do you get motion sick?
- Do you have a favorite billboard?
- Do you know what to do if there is a flat tire?
- Do you like a sun roof open?
- Do you like to eat in the car?
- Do you like to wear sun glasses in the car?
- Do you like toppings on your ice cream?
- Do you use public bathrooms?
- Did you bring your cell phone and does it have power?
- Do you have a form of identification with you?
- Have you ever been pulled over by a cop?
- Have you ever given money to a stranger on a road trip?
- Have you ever taken a road trip with animals?
- Have you ever went on a vacation alone?
- Have you ever run out of gas?

- If you could move to any place in the world, where would it be?
- If you could travel anywhere in the world, where would you travel?
- If you could travel in any vehicle, which one would it be?
- If you had three things to wish for from a magic genie, what would they be?
- If you have a driver's license, how many times did it take you to pass the test?
- What are you the most afraid of on vacation?
- What do you want to get away from the most when you are on vacation?
- What foods smells bad to you?
- What item to you bring on ever trip with you away from home?
- What makes you sleepy?
- What song would you love to hear on the radio when you're cruising on the highway?
- What travel job would you want the least?
- What will you miss most while you are away from home?
- What is something you always wanted to try?

- What is the best road side attraction that you ever saw?
- What is the farthest distance you ever biked?
- What is the farthest distance you ever walked?
- What is the weirdest thing you needed to buy while on vacation?
- What is your favorite candy?
- What is your favorite color car?
- What is your favorite family vacation?
- What is your favorite food in the world?
- What is your favorite gas station drink or food?
- What is your favorite license plate design?
- What is your favorite restaurant in the world?
- What is your favorite smell?
- What is your favorite song?
- What is your favorite sound that nature makes?
- What is your favorite thing to bring home from a vacation?
- What is your favorite vacation with friends?
- What is your favorite way to relax?

- What is your favorite weather conditions while driving?
- Where in the world would you rather never get to travel?
- Where is the farthest place you ever traveled in a car?
- Where is the farthest place you ever went North, South, East and West?
- Where is your favorite place in the world?
- Who is your favorite singer?
- Who taught you how to drive?
- Who will you miss the most while you are away?
- Who if the first person you will call when you get to your destination?
- Who brought you on your first vacation?
- Who likes to travel the most in your life?
- Would you rather be hot or cold?
- Would you rather drive above, below, or at the speed limited?
- Would you rather drive on a highway or a back road?
- Would you rather go on a train or a boat?
- Would you rather go to the beach or the woods?

NOTES

Made in United States
North Haven, CT
14 March 2023